DK SUPER Planet

FARMING
and Food Security

Farming is an essential part of life on our planet—learn about food security and the challenges presented to everyday farming

Produced for DK by
Editorial Just Content Limited
Design Studio Noel

Author Allison L. Hay

Senior Editor Amelia Jones
Senior Art Editor Gilda Pacitti
Managing Editor Katherine Neep
Managing Art Editor Sarah Corcoran
Production Editor Jaypal Chauhan
DTP Designer Rohit Singh
Production Controller Rebecca Parton
Publisher Sarah Forbes
Managing Director, Learning Hilary Fine

First American Edition, 2025
Published in the United States by DK Publishing,
a division of Penguin Random House LLC
1745 Broadway, 20th Floor, New York, NY 10019

Copyright © 2025 Dorling Kindersley Limited
25 26 27 28 29 10 9 8 7 6 5 4 3 2 1
001–345521–Apr/2025

All rights reserved.
Without limiting the rights under the copyright reserved
above, no part of this publication may be reproduced, stored
in or introduced into a retrieval system, or transmitted, in any
form, or by any means (electronic, mechanical, photocopying,
recording, or otherwise), without the prior written permission
of the copyright owner.
Published in Great Britain by Dorling Kindersley Limited

A catalog record for this book
is available from the Library of Congress.
HC ISBN: 978-0-5939-6598-6
PB ISBN: 978-0-5939-6597-9

DK books are available at special discounts when purchased
in bulk for sales promotions, premiums, fund-raising,
or educational use.
For details, contact: DK Publishing Special Markets,
1745 Broadway, 20th Floor, New York, NY 10019
SpecialSales@dk.com

Printed and bound in China

www.dk.com

This book was made with Forest Stewardship Council™ certified paper – one small step in DK's commitment to a sustainable future. **Learn more at www.dk.com/uk/information/sustainability**

Contents

What is Farming?	4
What is Food Security?	6
Different Types of Farm	8
Extreme Farming	10
Farming Challenges	12
Sustainable Farming	14
Organic Farming	16
Urban Farming	18
Vertical Farming	20
Floating Farming	22
Hydroponic Farming	24
Farming and the Environment	26
From Farm to Plate	28
Food Waste	30
Food Innovations	32
Everyday Science: Artificial Selection	34
Everyday Science: Gene Editing	36
Let's Experiment! Clever Composting	38
Let's Experiment! Grow Your Own Herbs	40
Vocabulary Builder: Growing Giant Vegetables	42
Glossary	44
Index	46

Words in **bold** are explained in the glossary on page 44.

What is FARMING?

Humans have been farming for at least 10,000 years. This means growing crops or raising **livestock**, like sheep and cows, for food. Farming made it easier to get food instead of hunting or **foraging**. This change had a huge impact on human society. Today, around 38 percent of Earth's surface is farmland. **Farms** are an essential part of modern life.

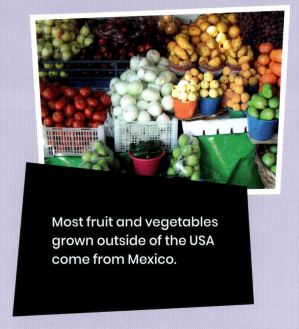

Most fruit and vegetables grown outside of the USA come from Mexico.

Bananas are one of the most popular fruits in the world. They are grown in more than 150 countries.

Fascinating fact

Some farmers grow soybeans. Oil from soybeans can be used to make crayons.

A ranch is a farm that raises livestock. King Ranch is the biggest farm in the USA. It covers more land than Rhode Island.

Over one-third of all US vegetables and three-quarters of all US fruit are grown in California due to its rich soil, ideal climate, and access to water.

Rice is the most valuable crop in the world. Most of the world's rice is grown in paddy fields in China.

People also farm fish. About half of the world's fish supply is farmed fish.

What is FOOD SECURITY?

There are around 570 million farms worldwide. They produce more than enough food to feed everyone on the planet. Regular access to **nutritious** food is known as **food security**, which is a human right. But there are some people and communities who do not have enough to eat. They do not know when they will get their next meal. These people are experiencing **food insecurity**.

The United Nations' zero hunger goal aims for a world where no one goes hungry. We can achieve this by increasing food security.

By 2050, the world population is expected to increase by 2 billion. Making food security a priority is essential as the population grows.

FOOD INSECURITY

One-third of all food produced is lost or wasted.

Almost half of the world's population cannot afford a healthy diet.

Poverty, climate change, and wars are major causes of global food insecurity.

SOLUTIONS TO FOOD INSECURITY

There are ways we can fight food insecurity. We can reduce the food we waste. We can teach people how to make nutritious meals.

Organizations like the World Bank spend billions of dollars each year tackling food insecurity around the world.

Fascinating fact

The United Nations declared 2013 the International Year of Quinoa (a grain-like seed) because of its potential to improve global food security.

Different Types of FARM

When we think of a farm, we might think of fruits and vegetables growing in orderly rows. But this is just one type of farm. This is known as an **arable farm**. You are also probably familiar with **pastoral farms**, which raise animals like cows and sheep. Mixed farms do both. But there are some more unusual farms out there, too.

Corn is the most widely grown crop in the world and is an important food for many people.

Farmers do not grow crops all the time. They have to let the soil take a break and recover the **nutrients** it loses. A field with no crops growing is called fallow land.

There are more than 700,000 ranches in the USA.

Edible land snails are high in protein, making them a valuable food source. These snails are farmed to provide food.

Most of the world's farmed fish are Atlantic salmon and rainbow trout. Fish are farmed in enclosures, like pens, in the sea.

Insect farms are an example of a more unusual type of farm. People farm insects such as crickets and mealworms for food. Insects such as silkworms and cochineal are farmed for materials (silk and red dye).

Fascinating fact

According to some sources, humans have been eating insects for 30,000 years.

Extreme FARMING

Some farms grow crops in extreme environments such as deserts, icy landscapes, or in built up cities. In **arid** climates it is hard for farmers to grow crops due to the hot, dry weather. Few plants will grow in very cold places without heat and shelter. The lack of outdoor space in cities means farmers are trying underground farming. All three types of extreme farms aim to increase food security for local people and communities.

Jordan is a very dry country. Almost three-quarters of it is desert. Water is scarce. This makes farming hard.

Farmers in hot, dry countries can use the resources they have to make farming possible, such as plenty of sunlight. This farm in Australia runs on solar energy and seawater. This means it will make more energy than it uses.

In very cold countries, farmers cannot grow crops in the open air. The temperatures are too extreme.

Find out!

Can you find out about any other extreme farms around the world?

The lack of space in urban areas means that some people are setting up farms underground. The first underground farm in the world was in London, UK. It was 108 ft (33 m) below the city streets.

Farming CHALLENGES

Farmers worldwide face many challenges that can kill or harm their crops. These challenges include bad weather, poor soil, pests, diseases, and climate change. When crops die or do not grow well, farmers have fewer crops to sell. This can lead to farms closing, which can make it harder for people to find food, increasing food insecurity.

Rwanda is a landlocked, hilly and mountainous country, which lacks water resources. This makes agricultural production unpredictable from one season to another.

Fascinating fact

Each year, 20 to 40 percent of all the crops grown in the world are lost due to pests.

Climate change impacts farmers in many ways. Extreme heat makes **harvesting** crops more dangerous. The **growing season** can be longer and result in poor crops.

Too much or too little rainfall can be devastating to farmers. Drought and floods can both kill crops or affect how well they grow.

Soil contains nutrients that plants need to grow. As farmers plant in soil again and again, the soil loses nutrients. This can lead to poor crops.

Crops can catch diseases, just like people. This can cause them to grow poorly or even die. Pests like exotic fruit flies can destroy entire crops.

Farmers use different strategies to fight these challenges. They plant a variety of crops in case some die. They collect rainwater in huge tanks to try to prevent flooding.

Sustainable FARMING

Industrial farming has only been around for a few hundred years. Yet its impact on the environment is huge. It can cause pollution and contribute to climate change. It can also kill plant and animal species.
In response to these challenges, people have developed **sustainable farming** methods. These methods use less energy and can help farmers save money.

Industrial farming works on a huge scale. It aims to grow the most crops or raise the most animals possible.

Biodiversity is the number of plant and animal species in an environment. Increasing biodiversity is an important goal of sustainable farmers.

Fascinating fact

Sweden, Japan, and Canada have the most sustainable agriculture in the world.

BOOSTING BIODIVERSITY
Farms with more biodiversity are more resilient against pests, disease, and extreme weather.

Sustainability is using some of Earth's resources without using them all. It does not harm people or the environment.

USING LIVESTOCK
Instead of keeping livestock in a separate area, farmers can raise them near crops. The animals provide fertilizer. The crops feed the animals.

ROTATING CROPS
Farmers rotate the crops they grow to help soil regain nutrients. This way, farmers can keep using the soil.

CARING FOR SOIL
Plowing leads to loss of soil, which is also called soil erosion. If farmers do not plow, less soil is lost. Using the right **fertilizers** can make the soil healthier.

Year 1
Year 2
Year 3
Year 4

Crop rotation

15

Organic FARMING

Sustainable farming is very similar to **organic farming**. Organic farmers use natural ways to control pests. They use natural fertilizers instead of artificial ones. Organic farming methods can reduce the loss of soil and make the soil healthier. It is not always more sustainable than **non-organic** farming. But many practices used by organic farmers are good for the environment.

Australia has the most organic farmland in the world. A lot of organic produce from Australia is exported to North America and Asia.

Governments regulate organic food. It has to meet certain standards to be certified. Otherwise, it cannot be called organic.

Organic farmers use **manure** and compost to fertilize plants. They do not use artificial fertilizers, as these harm the environment.

Artificial **pesticides** are not used by organic farmers. They use natural sources. These include bacteria, plant oils, or insects such as ladybugs and wasps.

Fascinating fact

One ladybug can eat up to 5,000 insects over the course of its life!

Animals that produce organic eggs and meat are free-range and have outdoor access.

Organic farmers grow fast-growing plants between crops. These plants add nutrients back into the soil. They prevent soil loss.

Urban FARMING

The countryside is not the only place where farming happens. It can also take place in cities. This is known as urban farming. Urban farming often makes use of spaces that would otherwise go unused, such as warehouses and rooftops. It is a great way to provide fresh, local produce to people, markets, and restaurants.

People practice urban farming in their own backyards. Some people raise and keep chickens.

Urban farms are also found in schools and community centers. They can be used to educate people about how to grow their own food.

Volunteers often run community gardens. They can grow fruit, vegetables, and flowers. There are hundreds of community gardens in Chicago, Illinois, in the USA.

Other urban farms grow crops to give people the ability to grow and eat their own food, even in the middle of a busy city.

Urban farms are also grown in warehouses or on rooftops. Nature Urbaine, in Paris, is a huge rooftop farm.

Find out!

Can you find out the names of any urban farms in your area?

Vertical FARMING

One way of making the best use of growing space is through **vertical farms**. These grow crops in rows stacked on top of each other. This means a lot of crops can grow in a small area. Cities are often home to them. They are a great way to ensure enough food can be grown for the community. They help increase food security worldwide.

Crops are often grown with no soil. The crops grow in water, using mist, or with the wastewater from fish farms instead.

Fascinating fact

Scientists at NASA are looking to develop vertical farming methods in space. This would give astronauts access to fresh salad and vegetables.

Crops need to be small and fast-growing to be farmed vertically. Otherwise, it is too expensive to farm them. Lettuce and strawberries grow very well vertically.

Vertical farms are often in unusual places, like shipping containers, old warehouses, and underground tunnels.

Tower Farm is a vertical farm in Chicago O'Hare International Airport. It can grow up to 1,100 plants at once.

Vertical farms grow indoors. Many use special lights, called LEDs, as their light source.

SpaceFarms is located in a hotel in the country of Georgia. It grows fresh produce for restaurants year-round.

Floating FARMING

Farmers in Rotterdam in the Netherlands have built the world's first floating dairy farm. Since it floats on water, it does not use any land space. Farmers can grow food locally, and people in the city can get fresh food. In India, floating farms go back many centuries. People can grow food during floods. Floating farms help tackle food insecurity.

The floating dairy has about 40 cows. They produce 320,000 liters of organic milk each year.

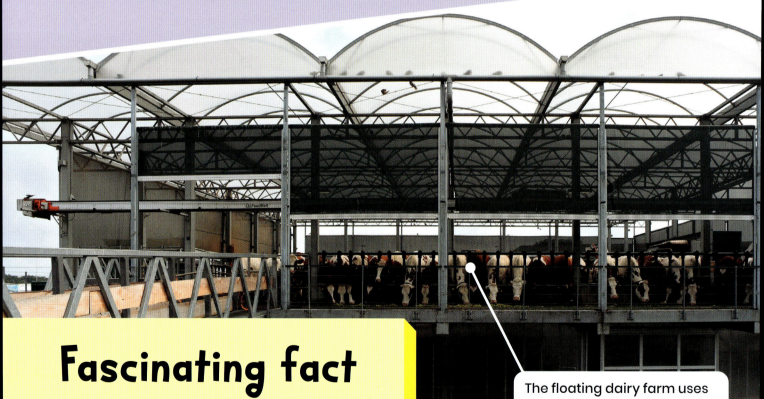

Fascinating fact

Floating farming is an ancient practice that originated in Bangladesh. Most of Bangladesh is wetland and experiences regular flooding.

The floating dairy farm uses sustainable methods. The cows eat bran, grass, and potato peelings, which are all waste products from the city.

Floating farms are only in a few areas of India. They do not cost much money to run. They also use sustainable materials.

Farmers can compost the materials used in floating farms after harvesting crops. This adds nutrients back into the soil.

There are some drawbacks. When the area is not flooded, people cannot use the farms. Snakes in the water can be a danger to farmers.

Hydroponic FARMING

Crops can be grown without any soil in **hydroponic farms**. They use nutrient-rich water instead. These farms are mostly indoors. They use artificial lights and watering systems. Even though they cost more money to run, hydroponic farms grow more food than traditional farms. They also grow crops more quickly. These farms can help to make sure that there is enough food for the community.

There are more than 2,300 hydroponic farms in the USA.

Find out!

Can you find out some diseases that affect hydroponic crops?

Some examples are: mildew, mold, root rot, viral diseases, and bacterial diseases.

Over one third of Earth's non-frozen land is taken up by traditional agriculture. Hydroponic farming, including vertical farming, can grow more food in less space.

Traditional agriculture uses almost three-quarters of the global water supply. Hydroponic farming uses 98 percent less water than traditional farms.

Critics say that hydroponic farms use a lot of electricity. They use more than seven times as much energy as a traditional greenhouse.

Hydroponic farms are controlled environments. This means that farmers can adjust growing conditions, like light and temperature, so crops thrive.

Farming and the ENVIRONMENT

Only some people believe that hydroponics is the future of farming. But many farmers want to move away from factory farming methods. Instead, some farmers use **regenerative agriculture**. It is similar to sustainable and organic farming methods. The focus is on improving the environment, not just food quality.

Many family farms use regenerative agriculture. Some grow their own **biofuel**. One farm in Arkansas has committed 4,000 acres (1,618 hectares) to conservation.

Fascinating fact

Soil is an amazing and little-understood **ecosystem**. One teaspoon of soil contains up to 6 billion **microorganisms**.

Hof Fuhlreit is a family farm in Germany. It combines **agroforestry** techniques with sustainable farm methods.

MAKING CARBON SINKS
Rice farmers introduce ducks to the paddies to eat weeds, control pests like snails, and put nutrients back in the soil.

Methods like crop cover can turn pastures and fields into **carbon sinks**. Carbon sinks store carbon dioxide, a **greenhouse gas**. This helps fight climate change.

HELPING ECOSYSTEMS
Not using pesticides allows pollinators like bees to thrive. Planting trees and cover crops, and reducing plowing means that the whole ecosystem is healthier and more diverse.

USING LIVESTOCK
Livestock are a big part of regenerative agriculture. As they move, they plow the land naturally. Grazing keeps crops in check. Their manure fertilizes the land.

MAKING MONEY
Healthier soil leads to more crops. Farmers earn more, and fewer farms may need to close.

From Farm to PLATE

The food we eat grows on farms and travels before it reaches our plates. We can buy local produce at markets, but other food comes from farther away. Farmers use different forms of transportation to deliver their produce to stores. Food is stored in refrigerators and freezers to keep it fresh. Some food comes from overseas by ships and airplanes.

Food that has a short shelf life is often transported by air. For example, asparagus and mangoes are moved between continents in airplanes.

Fascinating fact

Some vegetables travel more than 1,500 miles (2,414 km) to reach the dinner table.

FOOD TRANSPORTATION IN THE USA

Fresh produce is grown somewhere in the USA every month of the year.

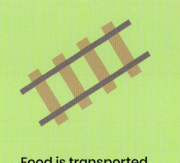

Food is transported within the USA along waterways, roads, and railroads.

Millions of tons of food are shipped between big states like California and New York.

Cold foods are shipped in exact temperatures in refrigerated trucks.

Strawberries have a shipping shelf life of one day. For potatoes, it is seven days.

The USA imports 15 percent of all its food from other countries.

Cargo ships and freight planes import food. 90 percent of all food trade is done by sea.

The USA imports 32 percent of all vegetables and 55 percent of all fruit that people eat.

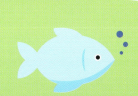

In the USA, about 90 percent of all seafood that people eat is imported.

Food WASTE

Food is wasted when it gets thrown away instead of eaten. This happens when food spoils or people do not eat what they buy. Even though many people face food insecurity, lots of food is wasted worldwide, costing money and harming the environment.

Almost half of all the food waste in the USA comes from households.

Find out!

Can you find out any ways that your community is reducing food waste?

Food waste is the source of around 10 percent of all greenhouse gas **emissions**. As the food breaks down, it releases greenhouse gases into the air.

Many supermarkets refuse to sell fruit and vegetables that are not perfect. Some have started to sell imperfect produce to fight food waste.

You can compost food waste. Composting reduces the amount of greenhouse gases released in the air. It also contributes to soil health.

Some food waste happens because people buy too much food. If you have food you cannot eat, you can donate it to a **food bank** before it goes bad.

Food
INNOVATIONS

Food is changing every day as scientists and researchers develop new technologies. Sometimes, this means making food in new ways. Other times, it focuses on improving people's health. New technologies can also help make sure everyone has enough to eat. **Artificial intelligence** can help improve food storage and reduce waste. This is a way to reduce food insecurity.

Robots can be used to deliver food to customers. In some warehouses, flying robots called drones are used to monitor food.

Factories allow lots of food to be produced to consistent standards, reducing wastage and reducing costs.

Fascinating fact

Scientists in New Zealand are working to develop lab-grown fruit with a taste and texture similar to fresh fruit.

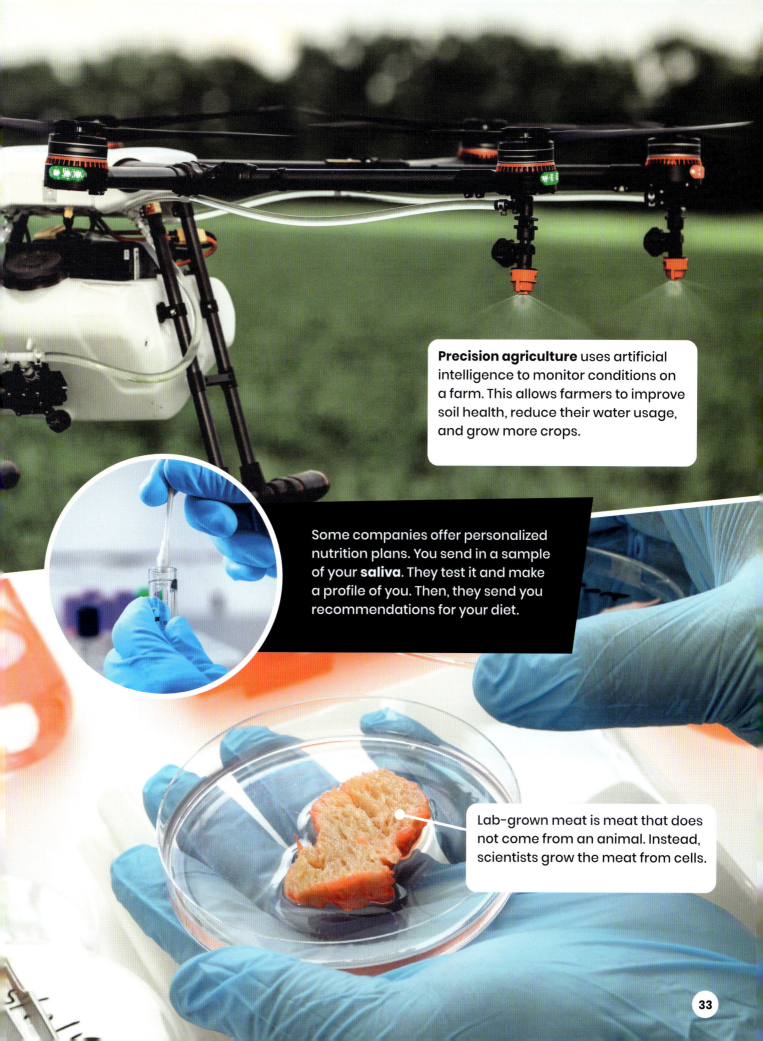

Precision agriculture uses artificial intelligence to monitor conditions on a farm. This allows farmers to improve soil health, reduce their water usage, and grow more crops.

Some companies offer personalized nutrition plans. You send in a sample of your **saliva**. They test it and make a profile of you. Then, they send you recommendations for your diet.

Lab-grown meat is meat that does not come from an animal. Instead, scientists grow the meat from cells.

Everyday SCIENCE
Artificial Selection

Farmers can change some crops to make them bigger, juicier, or sweeter. They do this by only planting seeds from crops they choose. Over time, all the crops they grow have the qualities they want. This is called **artificial selection**. Humans have used this process for thousands of years. Many of the fruits and vegetables we eat today result from artifical selection.

Wild mustard is a leafy vegetable. After thousands of years of artificial selection, it has given us vegetables including broccoli, cauliflower, and kale.

Fascinating fact

In the past, wild watermelons were small and bitter. Farmers selected the sweetest and juiciest ones to grow the watermelons we enjoy today.

Japanese scientists developed broccolini in the 1990s. It is a **hybrid** of broccoli and an Asian vegetable called gai lan.

Golden Delicious, Gala, and Braeburn apples are all 20th-century creations.

Carrots were not always orange. With time and artificial selection, white wild carrots became purple and yellow. Orange carrots came even later.

Corn was not always a delicious vegetable. Long ago, it was a grass. People in what is now Mexico used artificial selection over thousands of years to make corn what it is today.

Scientists have also developed hybrid fruits. Pluots are a cross between plums and apricots. Tayberries are a cross between a blackberry and a raspberry.

Everyday SCIENCE
Gene Editing

Today, scientists are looking for new ways to improve crops. One method is through **gene editing**. Unlike artificial selection, this is not something any farmer can practice. It has to be done in a lab by a trained scientist. It involves making tiny changes to a plant's **DNA**.

Scientists in the USA have edited soybeans. They have made them higher in **protein**. They have also made the soybeans grow in greater amounts.

In the UK, scientists have edited tomatoes to contain vitamin D. Vitamin D is vital for healthy bones and muscles.

Crop editing is being used in the fight against climate change. Scientists can edit crops to tolerate drought and flooding better.

Crops like rice can be infected by fungal diseases. Higher temperatures as a result of climate change will bring more diseases like this and more pests. Gene editing crops and livestock could give them more resistance to these challenges.

Scientists are also working on ways to make people like healthy food more. They are learning how to improve flavors and textures.

Food security is an issue around the world. Editing crops like bananas can make them more nutritious.

Let's EXPERIMENT!

CLEVER COMPOSTING

For crops to grow strong, they must be planted in healthy soil with plenty of nutrients. Farmers can keep their soil healthy by mixing in compost made from food scraps and old plants. Some farmers use fertilizers that contain artificial ingredients. Compost is a natural way to keep soil healthy and reuse waste.

You will need:
- A pen
- A plastic container with lid
- A paintbrush and acrylic paint
- Dead leaves
- Old coffee grounds
- Eggshells
- Fruit and vegetable scraps
- Cardboard and newspaper

Be careful when making holes in the container. You can ask an adult to help.

1 Use a pen to make holes in the lid of the plastic container. Use paint to decorate your container.

2 Put the leaves, coffee grounds, eggshells, fruit and vegetable scraps, cardboard, and newspaper in the container.

3 Put the lid on your container. Leave it outside for a few months.

4 Over time, the items in your container will break down to form compost! You can sprinkle compost on plants to help them grow.

SALAD CROPS AT PLAW HATCH FARM

Plaw Hatch Farm in the UK uses compost to grow organic food. It is a mixed farm with cows, sheep, pigs, chickens, and arable crops. The farm has used sustainable practices for over 40 years. It is open to visitors so that people can learn more about food production.

Let's EXPERIMENT!

GROW YOUR OWN HERBS

You do not need to be a farmer to grow your own food! Growing herbs is easy and fun using a few simple materials. You just need some containers, soil, and seeds. You can grow herbs like basil, mint, or parsley on your windowsill.

You will need:
- Empty juice cartons
- Scissors
- A pen
- Large paper clips
- Compost
- Stones
- Different herb seeds
- Water

Be careful when cutting and making holes in the cartons. You can ask an adult to help..

1 Save some empty juice cartons. Rinse them out. Cut the top off each carton. Use a pen to make drainage holes in the bottom.

2 Join the cartons with paper clips. Put some stones in each one and add compost.

3 Sprinkle different herb seeds in each carton. Cover the seeds with more compost and add water.

4 Keep your cartons somewhere sunny. Water them regularly until they are ready to eat!

A FARMER'S MARKET IN OREGON

Farmers work hard to grow fresh food such as fruits, vegetables, and grains, helping make sure we have enough healthy food to eat. You can find their produce at markets and in grocery stores. Some food has been grown locally, but some produce comes from farther away, including overseas.

Vocabulary BUILDER
Growing Giant Vegetables

Farmers around the world raise crops. Some farmers grow giant vegetables. They hope to break records and win medals. Read this article discussing how they do it.

RECORD-BREAKING VEGETABLES!

By Agriculture Reporter

How do farmers achieve record-breaking sizes? According to one farmer, it's nothing special.

They start by **sowing** quality seeds. If the seeds **germinate**, the farmers take care of the **seedlings**.

Plants need high-quality soil full of nutrients and plenty of water. They also need a long growing season to get as big as possible. This means farmers sow seeds in the spring, so they have many months to grow before the fall harvest.

One of the most challenging parts of the competition is transporting the giant produce in one piece. As the massive vegetables grow and ripen, they get softer. The last thing a farmer wants is a sunken pumpkin or a smashed cucumber.

And what do the farmers do with their giant **specimens** after the competition? They eat them!

Things in a garden compost, gloves, greenhouse, hose, nutrients, pests, rainwater, season, shears, shovel, soil, trowel, water, watering can, wheelbarrow

What gardeners do add fertilizer, dig, drain, germinate, grow, harvest, mow, plant, prepare, prune, pull weeds, rake, sow seeds, till, trim

Tim Saint's cabbage weighs in at 52 pounds (23.7 kg)!

Ron Root shows off his winning 1,535 pound (696 kg) pumpkin!

Your friend wants to start a vegetable garden. What advice can you give them? Use the words in the word box above and the example on page 42 to write a letter and tell them what they should do to care for their garden.

Glossary

Agroforestry A way of farming that combines growing trees with growing crops or rearing livestock.

Arable farms Farms that grow crops.

Arid Very dry without much rainfall.

Artificial intelligence The ability of computers and machines to perform tasks in a similar way to how humans think and learn.

Artificial selection The process in which farmers choose plants or animals to breed together so that they get a new plant or animal with the qualities they want.

Biofuel A fuel made from plants or other living things.

Carbon neutral Where the amount of carbon dioxide being given out is the same as the amount being used.

Carbon sinks A natural place, such as a forest, that takes in carbon from the air.

DNA A special code inside every living thing that gives instructions on how their body should work. It helps decide things like your eye color or how tall you are.

Ecosystem A community of living things that interact with non-living things in their environment.

Emissions Gases and substances released into the air.

Farm An area or piece of land where people grow crops or raise animals.

Fertilizers Substances added to soil to help crops and plants grow better.

Food banks Places that collect and provide food for people who are not getting enough nutritious food to eat.

Food security Having enough nutritious food to eat.

Food insecurity Not having regular access to enough nutritious food.

Foraging Searching for food, like nuts, berries, mushrooms, and plants that grow in the wild.

Genes The instructions that tell living things how to grow and work.

Gene editing Making tiny changes to the genes inside living things, like plants, animals, or even people, to help them work better.

Germinate The process in which a seed starts to grow into a plant.

Greenhouse gas A gas in Earth's atmosphere that traps heat from the Sun and warms our planet.

Growing season The time of year when the weather conditions are best to help plants grow.

Harvest A time when farmers can pick or cut their crops once they are fully grown.

Hybrid The offspring of two different species of plants or animals.

Hydroponic farms Farms that grow crops using nutrient-rich water instead of soil.

Livestock Domestic animals that people keep for food, milk, wool, or leather.

Manure Animal poop from cows and other livestock that is used to fertilize crops.

Microorganisms Living things that are so small you cannot see them, such as bacteria, fungi, and algae.

Non-organic Used to describe produce that is grown with the use of artificial chemicals.

Nutrients Substances in soil that help it stay healthy.

Nutritious Food that helps your body work.

Organic Used to describe produce that is grown naturally, without the use of any artificial chemicals.

Pastoral farms Farms that rear livestock such as cows and sheep.

Pesticides Chemicals used to kill or control pests.

Pollution The process of releasing harmful things into the environment.

Precision agriculture Farming that uses technology to help produce food more effectively.

Regenerative agriculture Farming that helps improve the health of the soil and the surrounding environment.

Saliva The clear liquid in the mouth made of water and other chemicals, also known as spit.

Seedling A young plant that has just started to grow from a seed.

Sowing Planting seeds in the soil to grow crops.

Specimens Examples of things.

Sustainability Using resources such as water and energy without using them up to make sure there are enough for the future.

Sustainable farming Farming that protects the environment by using natural methods, making sure there are enough resources such as water and energy for the future.

Vertical farms Farms where crops are grown stacked on top of one another, often in indoor buildings.

Index

A
apples 35
arable farms 8
Arkansas 26
artificial intelligence 32, 33
artificial selection 34–35
Australia 10, 16

B
bananas 4, 37
Bangladesh 22
biodiversity 14, 15
biofuel 26
broccolini 34

C
cabbages 43
California 4
Canada 14
carbon sinks 27
carrots 35
challenges to farming 12–13
Chicago 19
chickens 17, 18
China 5
climate change 13, 37
community gardens 19
composting 23, 31, 38–39
corn 8, 35
crop rotation 15

D
dairies, floating 22
diseases 13, 24, 37

E
environment 26–27
experiments
    composting 38–39
    growing herbs 40–41
extreme farming 10–11

F
factories 32
fallow land 8
famine 7
farming
    defined 4–5
    traditional 24–25
fish farms 5, 9, 20
floating farming 22–23
food security, defined 6–7
fruit 4, 5, 29
    hybrid 35
    innovations 32
    waste 31

G
gene editing 36–37
greenhouse gases 27, 30

H
herbs, growing 40–41
Hof Fuhlreit farm 26
humans, and insects 9
hybrid fruits 35
hydroponic farming 24–25

I
India 23
industrial farming 14
innovations 32–33
insect farms 9

J
Japan 14
Jordan 10

K
King Ranch 5

L
ladybugs 17
lettuce 20
livestock 4, 5, 15
diseases 37
    and regenerative agriculture 30
London 11

M
markets 41
meat 17, 33
Mexico 4, 35

N
NASA 20
Nature Urbaine 19
New Zealand 32

O
Oregon 41
organic farming 16–17

P
Paris 19
pastoral farms 8
pesticides 17, 27
pests 12, 13, 16, 17, 37
Plaw Hatch Farm 39
pluots 35
population, world 6
precision agriculture 33
pumpkins 43

R
rainfall 13
ranches 5, 8
regenerative agriculture 26
rice 5, 27, 37
robots 32
Rotterdam 22

S
snails 9
snakes 23
soil 8, 13, 15, 26
    and composting 31
    and organic farming 16, 17
soybeans 4, 36
SpaceFarms 21
strawberries 20
sustainable 14–15
sustainable farming 14–15, 26
Sweden 14

T
tayberries 35
technologies 32–33
tomatoes 36
Tower Farm 21
traditional farming 24–25
transportation 28–29

U
underground farms 11
United Nations 6
urban farming 18–19

V
vegetables 4, 5
    artificial selection 34–35
    and food waste 30–31
    giant 42–3
    journey to dinner table 28, 29
vertical farming 20–21
vitamin D 36

W
waste, food 7, 30–31, 32
watermelons 34
wild mustard 34

Acknowledgments

The publisher would like to thank the following for their kind permission to reproduce their photographs:

(Key: a-above; b-below/bottom; c-center; f-far; l-left; r-right; t-top)

Adobe Stock: Around Ball 18-19bc, Industrieblick 32b, Jacob Lund 16bl, Chuck Place 35tr, Richard 31tl; **Alamy Stock Photo**: Agencja Fotograficzna Caro / Schnitger 21tl, Mark Andrews 10-11b, Associated Press / Brian Kersey 19tl, Stefano Mazzola / Awakening 32cra, Arunabh Bhattacharjee 23tr, Santanu Bose 23br, Alan Bramley 27br, Cavan Images 18tr, CBW 16-17b, Lorne Chapman 28, B Christopher 31bl, Hilda DeSanctis 27bl, DPA Picture Alliance 26bc, Randy Duchaine 18, Lincoln Fowler 10, Global Press 23l, Sarah M. Golonka 27ca, Greatstock / Michael Edwards 35bl, Simon Hadley 30br, John D. Ivanko 21r, Frans Lemmens 14, Maxppp / Photopqr / Le Parisien / Olivier Lejeune 19r, PA Images / Aaron Chown 43cr, Ian Rutherford 14br, UPI / Terry Schmitt 43clb, Adrian Weston 26cra, ZUMA Press, Inc. / Martin Bertrand 22tr; **Dreamstime.com**: Alisonh29 15t, Anthonyata 5tr, Anzebizjan 37tl, Yuri Arcurs 15tl, Arhivafoto15 24cr, Artiemedvedev 13tl, Artifexorlova 15cr, Aruna1234 34crb, 35crb, Woraphon Banchobdi 8b, Belyjmishka 33t, Bizoon 8br, Bluetoes67 16-17tc, Bobbrooky 6bl, David Buechner 4tr, Carriel313 27tl, Tiziano Casalta 12b, Angelo Cordeschi 34b, Gilles Decruyenaere 17tr, Elena Elisseeva 4, Vladislav Gajic 9tl, Vadim Ginzburg 25tr, Grigorenko 35tl, Kerry Hill 13bl, Isgalkin84 9tr, Kenishirotie 24bl, James Kirkikis 5tl, Dusan Kostic 36tr, Ksya 21bl, Lianem 35br, Lightpoet 8clb, Lunamarina 4br, Homi Maki 37tr, Simone Matteo Giuseppe Manzoni 10tr, Marbury67 17bl, Oleh Marchak 13clb, Markit 36clb, Aleksandr Medvedkov 14tr, Meunierd 27tr, Krisztian Miklosy 11clb, Velichka Miteva 13cla, Mulderphoto 24-25bc, Nitsuki 15bl, Nuvisage 9b, Natalia Oskanova 30cra, Photoallel 16cr, Photomall 25br, Pojoslaw 18bc, Ppy2010ha 33b, Zbigniew Ratajczak 34cra, Sifian Hayu Lucky Riyanto 24-25tc, Ronstik 33cl, Dzmitry Sianko 36b, Stevanovicigor 13r, Stockcube 30b, Siraphob Tatiyarat 5br, Alexander Traksel 37br, Vadreams 21cl, Dmytro Varavin 6br, Bruce Whittingham 31r, Wirestock 20, Lei Xu 5bl, Yulan 26b; **Getty Images**: AFP / John Thys 22b, Moment / Daniel Haug 11t; **Getty Images / iStock**: E+ / Dusan Ilic 37bl; **Shutterstock.com**: Arthur Greenberg 28tr

Cover images: *Front:* **Dreamstime.com**: Ifeelstock t, Suvit Maka br; **Shutterstock.com**: B Brown bl, Golden Sikorka cr; *Back:* **Alamy Stock Photo**: Arunabh Bhattacharjee bl; **Dreamstime.com**: Gilles Decruyenaere tl, Vadim Ginzburg cl